FBI HOSTAGE RESCUE & SWAT TEAMS

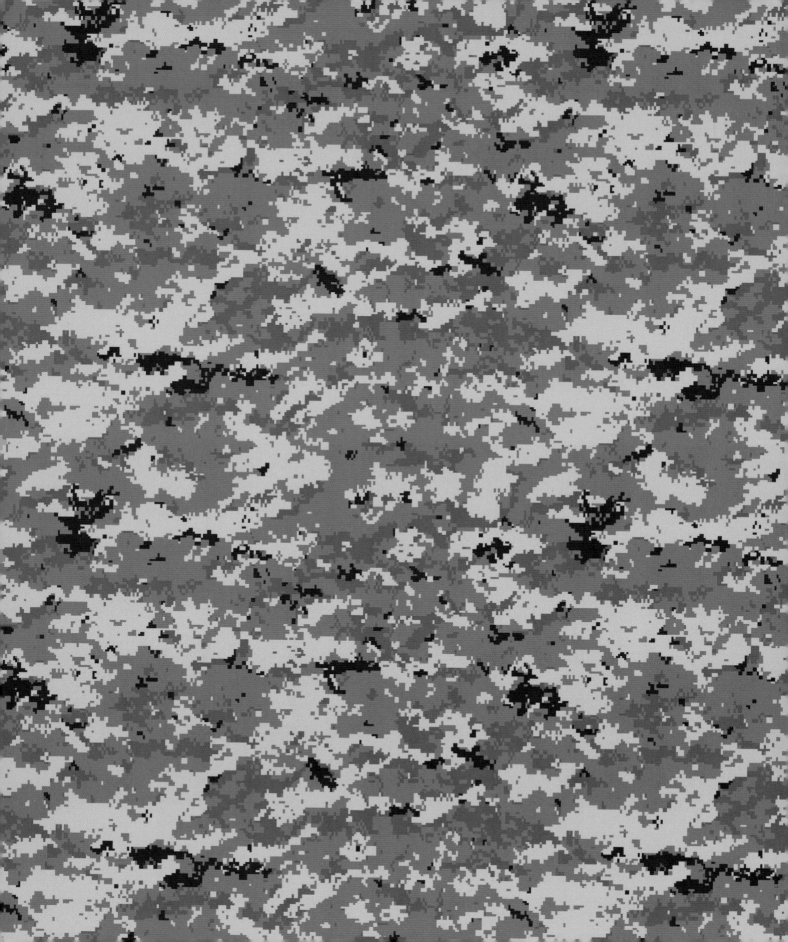

U.S. SPECIAL FORCES

FBI HOSTAGE RESCUE & SWAT TEAMS

JIM WHITING

CREATIVE
PAPER BACKS

PUBLISHED BY Creative Paperbacks

P.O. Box 227, Mankato, Minnesota 56002

Creative Paperbacks is an imprint of The Creative Company

www.thecreativecompany.us

DESIGN AND PRODUCTION BY Christine Vanderbeek

ART DIRECTION BY Rita Marshall

PRINTED IN the United States of America

PHOTOGRAPHS BY

Alamy (Alliance Images, Chuck Eckert, Images of Africa Photobank, SCPhotos, Marmaduke St. John), Corbis (David Brabyn, Anna Clopet, Rauchwetter/dpa, PHILIP SEARS/Reuters, Greg Smith, Gary Stewart/AP, Nick Ut/AP), Getty Images (Patrick AVENTURIER/Gamma-Rapho), iStockphoto (icholakov, qingwa, spxChrome), Shutterstock (ALMAGAMI, gst, trekandshoot), SuperStock (Marka)

LIBRARY OF CONGRESS CATALOGING-IN-PUBLICATION DATA

Whiting, Jim.

FBI hostage rescue & SWAT teams / Jim Whiting.

p. cm. — (U.S. Special Forces)

Includes bibliographical references and index.

Summary: A chronological account of the American special forces unit known as FBI S.W.A.T., including key details about important figures, landmark missions, and controversies.

ISBN 978-1-60818-462-0 (HARDCOVER)

ISBN 978-1-62832-048-0 (PBK)

1. United States. Federal Bureau of Investigation. Hostage Rescue Team—Juvenile literature. 2. Hostages—Juvenile literature. 3. Rescues—Juvenile literature. I. Title.

HV8144.F43W458 2014

363.2'3—dc23   2013036171

CCSS: RI.5.1, 2, 3, 8; RH.6-8.4, 5, 6, 8

FIRST EDITION

9 8 7 6 5 4 3 2 1

U.S. SPECIAL FORCES

TABLE OF CONTENTS

FORCE FACTS Minimum physical standards for HRT training are 12 pull-ups, 60 sit-ups, 50 pushups, swimming 200 meters in 7 minutes, and running 2 miles (3.2 km) in less than 15 minutes.

Students train at the FBI Academy campus located south of Washington, D.C.

INTRODUCTION

IN 1980, CUBAN PRESIDENT FIDEL CASTRO ALLOWED MORE than 100,000 of his people to come to the United States in a mass emigration event known as the Mariel Boatlift. Several thousand were dangerous criminals whom Castro wanted to get rid of. Many committed crimes in the U.S. and were imprisoned. Threatened with deportation to Cuba in 1991, dozens of those *Marielitos* housed in the Federal Correctional Facility in Talladega, Alabama, seized control of part of the prison and took 10 hostages.

The Hostage Rescue Team (HRT) of the Federal Bureau of Investigation (FBI) quickly responded, as did other federal forces. During an uneasy truce that lasted for more than a week, little progress was made in resolving the situation. At that point, authorities became convinced the hostages were in danger of being killed. HRT was ordered to retake the facility.

The operation began in the early morning darkness when HRT members blew open several doors. Rushing inside, they flung stun grenades to momentarily blind their targets. The grenades also generated a shock wave that knocked down anyone in the area. Moments later, the assault team threw "stingers," which unleashed dozens of painful rubber pellets, and fog-causing devices that also emitted a skin-irritating chemical.

"It was loud, confused, and smoky," said one team member. "It seemed like we caught them completely by surprise. There were no attempts to fight back." From start to finish, the operation took just three minutes. The hostages were unharmed, and the only *casualty* was a slightly wounded prisoner.

Communist leader Fidel Castro strictly regulated who could enter and exit Cuba.

HOSTAGES AND HANDCUFFS

U.S. SPECIAL FORCES

When people think of special forces, they might envision U.S. Navy SEALs taking down America's most wanted man, Osama bin Laden, in 2011. Or the army's Green Berets, whose jaunty headgear visually sets them apart from other military units. Or Delta Force, the ultra-secret unit that has often been featured in movies, television, and thriller novels.

However, these highly skilled warriors can't operate on American soil. The Posse Comitatus Act, which dates back to 1878, forbids using the military for civilian law enforcement, unless the president specifically allows it. Yet long before the 9/11 terrorist attacks in 2001, the need for operators able to take on terrorists—either homegrown or from abroad—who threaten people inside the U.S. became apparent.

The first inkling of danger came at the 1972 Olympic Games in Munich, West Germany, when terrorists murdered 11 members of the Israeli team inside the Olympic Village. Terror struck much closer to home five years later. A group of gunmen took over 3 buildings in Washington, D.C., and held more than 100 hostages for 38 hours. The situation was resolved with minimal loss of life, but it illustrated the need for more advanced skills than local police possessed. "It would have been a bloodbath," said Donald Bassett, an FBI firearms instructor. "These [police] officers had never been training to do airborne assaults."

The FBI of the mid-1970s had a number of Special Weapons and Training (SWAT) teams at its disposal. These were modeled after the Los Angeles Police Department's SWAT teams, which first formed in 1967. Eventually, each of the 56 FBI field offices would have its own SWAT team, consisting of special agents

The 1972 killings inside the Olympic Park became known as the Munich Massacre.

FORCE FACTS HRT operators often "ride the skids" of their helicopters, standing on the narrow rails that serve as landing gear. They jump off when the aircraft lands.

who undertake SWAT training in addition to their other duties. But even the best SWAT teams couldn't keep up with the increasing firepower and boldness of terrorist groups.

By the early 1980s, the need for a highly skilled force capable of launching "airborne assaults" and other antiterrorist actions was becoming more apparent. Four major events were on the docket in 1984: the Republican and Democratic national conventions, the World's Fair in New Orleans, Louisiana, and especially the Summer Olympics in Los Angeles. All these events were potential terrorist magnets. "When Los Angeles won the nomination for the 1984 Olympics, the question was, 'Who would handle an event such as Munich?' And there weren't a lot of good answers. That's how the idea of a Hostage Rescue Team evolved," said FBI deputy director Sean Joyce, a former HRT member.

The HRT initiative got a big boost when then FBI Director William Webster visited the Delta Force training facility at Fort Bragg, North Carolina, late in 1981. He was impressed by the professionalism and efficiency the operators demonstrated. But when he talked with the men afterward, he noticed that they seemed to be missing one key piece of law-enforcement equipment. An operator explained the apparent omission: "We put two rounds in their forehead. The dead don't need handcuffs."

Delta's lack of handcuffs concerned Webster. He wanted a dedicated unit that trained full-time and would be capable of *deploying* anytime and anywhere in the country on short notice. He also wanted a unit that was aware of the principles of law enforcement and of constitutional requirements for making arrests. "They are FBI agents first and foremost, and they have the ability to perform special agent duties—whether it's obtaining evidence or interviewing an individual—anywhere in the world while being able to operate in all types of environments, no matter how inhospitable," Joyce added.

Final approval for Webster's plan came early in 1982, with 89

Riding the skids allows operators to save time and engage an enemy more quickly.

FORCE FACTS Supervisors of a training exercise often alter the nature of the exercise after it starts so that operators learn how to change plans in an instant and adapt to changing conditions.

men and 1 woman selected for initial training. Fifty continued on for advanced training. In planning the training regimen, the FBI drew on the expertise of American military forces and similar organizations around the world. One particularly influential special operations unit was the French National Gendarmerie Intervention Group (Groupe d'Intervention de la Gendarmerie Nationale, or GIGN). One of GIGN's leaders explained that their mission was simply "to save lives." That quickly became the new American group's motto.

Choosing a name to reflect its life-saving mission was crucial for the new unit. "Super-SWAT," the initial choice, sounded too elitist to some. "Hostage Rescue Team" struck a better note, but the name may be somewhat misleading. "Rescuing hostages is but a part of the full range of capabilities that we train and are prepared to respond to," said HRT director Steve Fiddler in 2009. Future operations would involve hijackings, manhunts, high-profile arrests, protecting dignitaries, and dealing with extremist groups in addition to actual hostage situations.

As the members of the unit neared the end of their training late in 1983, they faced one final exercise, this time a scenario involving "terrorists" who threatened to detonate a nuclear device hidden somewhere in New Mexico's Kirtland Air Force Base near Albuquerque. They had also seized a number of hostages and taken them to a remote cabin. The FBI promptly sent HRT to the scene. As negotiations with the concealed terrorists continued during the following three days, the team managed to learn the location of the hideout. They also discovered where the bomb was.

HRT focused on the hideout, and a SWAT team was tasked with recovering the bomb. Timing was critical. Both teams had to strike

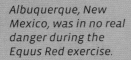

Albuquerque, New Mexico, was in no real danger during the Equus Red exercise.

at exactly the same moment, neutralizing the nuclear device while preserving the lives of the hostages. HRT operators forced down the doors of the hideout, tossed in flash-bang grenades to stun the terrorists, and fanned out inside. In less than 30 seconds, every *tango* was gunned down. All the hostages were safe. And the weapon didn't detonate.

This operation served as the newly minted HRT's "final exam" and was code-named "Equus Red." Soon afterward, HRT went active. Its first deployment was to the Olympics, which went off without any problems. The following year, a group of *white supremacists* living in a compound in the Ozark Mountains of Arkansas shot two state troopers during a traffic stop. HRT conducted several nighttime operations to gather intelligence, and then—in tandem with several FBI SWAT teams—stormed part of the compound. Negotiations eventually led to the surrender of the entire group. A search revealed a *cache* of military-grade weapons and drums of *cyanide* the group's members had planned on pouring into a nearby city's water supply.

The unit's reputation took a hit after a pair of highly

SWAT teams enter locked rooms by using explosives, battering rams, or ballistics.

publicized cases in Idaho and Texas a few months apart in 1992 and 1993 resulted in the deaths of several dozen people. The outcome illustrated the need for a unified command to oversee all aspects of future situations. The Critical Incident Response Group (CIRG) was established to bring all the FBI's crisis management units together. One element of CIRG was the Tactical Support Branch, which includes HRT as well as SWAT teams.

The new approach received its first major test in 1996, when an armed confrontation with members of the Montana Freemen began. The group rejected the authority of the federal government in favor of its own system. A bank tried to foreclose on the land the group occupied, but the Freemen refused to leave. The FBI also had arrest warrants out for several men on the site. This time, the situation was resolved after an 81-day, injury-free standoff.

Since its beginnings, HRT has become involved in more than 800 actions. The majority of them were either secret or resolved peacefully, thereby remaining virtually unknown to the general public. One notable exception came early in 2013. A 65-year-old retired trucker in Midland, Alabama, shot and killed a school-bus driver, kidnapped a 5-year-old boy, and held him hostage in a heavily fortified underground bunker. After a tense, six-day standoff that drew national attention, HRT operators raided the bunker. They killed the trucker and rescued the boy unharmed. Once again, the unit proved worthy of its motto: To Save Lives.

FBI operators arrived on the scene soon after a young Alabama boy was taken hostage.

FORCE FACTS In HRT's 30-year history, fewer than 300 men have been operators.

MAKING THE CUT

U.S. SPECIAL FORCES

TRADITIONALLY, APPLYING TO HRT HAS BEEN OPEN TO ALL FBI special agents with a minimum of three years' field experience, consistently superior performance evaluations, and a willingness to serve at least three years in the unit. Even though HRT is one of the most coveted assignments in the FBI, its combination of high qualifying standards and demanding lifestyle resulted in its understaffing for many years. So in 2007, the FBI instituted the Tactical Recruitment Program (TRP) to increase the pool of potential operators. TRP now allows agents who have three years' experience in military combat or law-enforcement SWAT to apply for the HRT program with a commitment to two years in the field.

While candidates have many reasons for applying, former HRT member Christopher Whitcomb echoed the feelings of many when he wrote, "HRT represented something almost mythically grand. Every time something big happened in the United States, HRT flew in, strapped on black *Nomex* flight suits and submachine guns, and straightened it out. This is it, I thought." Jaime Atherton, a member of the original team in 1983, added, "The challenge that was involved, the chance to be a part of something new, and the ability to make a difference—that's why I joined the Bureau."

Once they decide to join, all applicants must take the two-week HRT selection course, which is held twice a year at the FBI

Dangerous assignments and training exercises make qualifying standards high for HRT agents.

Academy in Quantico, Virginia. The first day begins before dawn and includes a series of runs, swims, multistory stair climbs, and other strenuous physical activities. Sometimes trainees are required to perform these tasks while wearing a vest weighing more than 50 pounds (22.7 kg) and carrying a 35-pound (15.9 kg) battering ram. And that's the easy day. "The process is designed to identify individuals who will perform the best in a crisis situation," said Sean Joyce. "The point is to break you down to see how you perform under stress."

To assist in the breaking-down process, trainees must ascend a rock wall and then climb a narrow ladder to a point more than 70 feet (21.3 m) high. They are required to paddle a rubber boat across a lake as a helicopter tilted on its side blows wind and waves against the craft. One of the primary objectives of such tests is to ensure that potential operators have a great deal of upper-body strength. As Danny Coulson, the original leader of HRT, explained in his book *No Heroes*, "We focused heavily on upper-body and hand strength because commanders at Delta, SEAL Team Six, and the European services had all told us that it was an operator's most important physical attribute. Often the most difficult part of a counterterrorist operation was not the fight itself but getting to the scene in the first place. That could involve climbing, jumping, swimming, running, crawling, walking, or *fast-roping* out of helicopters. All these required extraordinary upper-body strength." As of yet, no woman has become an HRT operator in the field.

At least as important as the physical challenges are the mental and psychological ones that HRT operatives face. Selectees never know what is coming up next, so they have to be flexible in adjusting to each test as it arises. In addition, they never know how they are performing in the eyes of their instructors, or even to what standards they are being held. This uncertainty creates additional stress.

HRT and SWAT members must be physically fit and ready for any hostile situation.

Those who ace the selection course report to the New Operator Training School (NOTS) at the FBI Academy. The NOTS has nearly 24 buildings, including dormitories, classrooms, offices, an auditorium, gym, swimming pool, and weight room. It also has firing ranges, an outdoor track, and other facilities.

For the next eight months, the men are immersed in an increasingly demanding regimen that both enhances existing individual skills and introduces them to new ones such as scuba diving and fast-roping. Their training also integrates them as members of a team, but always, the emphasis is on speed. In hostage situations, even a few seconds can make the difference between life and death.

One of the most important facilities at the NOTS is the Tactical Firearms Training Center (TFTC). Its moveable walls can be reconfigured to mimic a variety of environments that operators are likely to face. The interior walls are rubber-lined to absorb bullet fragments, eliminating the potential for ricocheting. Most of the sides are open so that the smoke from flashbang grenades and firing thousands of rounds of ammunition is quickly dispersed. Inside the center is a mockup of a commercial jetliner, which includes dozens of seated mannequins and pre-recorded screams and gunfire to add to the realism. Overhead are a series of catwalks equipped with microphones and cameras. Instructors can directly observe the action and examine the feeds to respond to the trainees' performance.

A four-story tower at one end of the TFTC overlooks the rest of the structure. It is outfitted with interior and exterior stairways, allowing for a variety of types of training such as fast-roping, *rappelling*, and hoisting gear. Another key facility on the campus is "Hogan's Alley," a 10-acre (4 ha) simulated

Quantico's FBI National Academy trains local and international law enforcement officers.

SWAT members practice approaching a criminal target at a California training facility.

town with homes, a bank, a post office, and other elements of contemporary urban life. Actors portray "townspeople" from innocent bystanders to cutthroat terrorists. Trainees gain real-world experience by engaging in house-to-house combat.

The training course culminates in a full-scale hostage rescue exercise—such as Equus Red—to test everything the trainees have learned. If they succeed, then they become full-fledged HRT operators. Yet their training isn't over. From this point until they leave the team, operators continue to train. For at least five days a week, they constantly hone their skills to make their responses as automatic as possible. Even a seemingly minor task such as changing the *magazines* on their weapons can always be improved upon, saving a precious second or two.

On most days, time is set aside for physical conditioning, to maintain and improve strength and stamina. Gear maintenance and team planning sessions are also important. But the foundation of all training is close quarters combat (CQC), firearms,

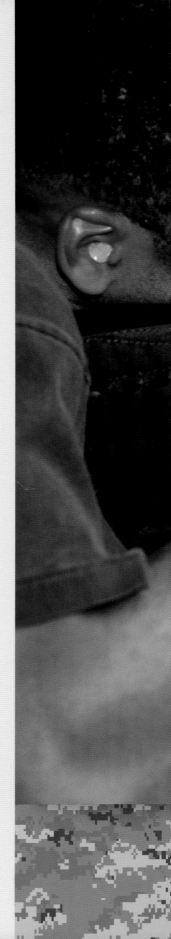

and sniper training. "Those are our core skill sets," said Charles Pierce, commander of one of the HRT units. "The other things are built around that."

Operators fall into one of two groups: assaulters or sniper/observers. Operators selected as sniper/observers train at the Marine Corps' elite Scout/Sniper School, where they learn concealment techniques and target *reconnaissance* in addition to enhancing their shooting skills. Assaulters often specialize in such areas as *breaching*, communications, and treating serious wounds.

One of the most vital aspects of engaging in ongoing training involves coordinating the efforts of the snipers and assaulters. Snipers sneak into advanced positions, where they often lie almost motionless for hours as they keep in radio contact with the rest of the team. Then it's "go" time. Snipers provide covering fire for the assault team, which moves in and kills or disables the targets as quickly and efficiently as possible. If there are hostages, the goal is to rescue them unharmed. To pull off such a difficult task successfully, the squads need to continually practice coordinating their efforts.

The same general philosophy of "saving lives" underlies FBI SWAT teams. To be eligible, field agents must have a minimum of two years' service. Potential members must pass a pistol qualification course and physical fitness test, plus a psychological evaluation. Once accepted for their respective teams, they undergo refresher training two to four times per month. Several times a year they undergo a more extensive exercise, often utilizing vacant houses that the owners have made available for their use.

All HRT and SWAT team members must be proficient with firearms such as pistols, shotguns, and rifles.

FORCE FACTS In total, about 1,100 agents belong to SWAT teams, a little less than 10 percent of the nearly 14,000 special agents working for the FBI.

THE CALL COMES IN, AND HRT GOES OUT

AT ANY TIME OF DAY OR NIGHT, "THE CALL"—A SITUATION beyond the scope and capabilities of local law enforcement and with the possibility of becoming life-threatening—comes in to HRT headquarters at Quantico. Immediately, the scene becomes an extremely well-organized beehive of activity. The men have been through this scenario many times, both during training exercises and in real-life missions. Team leaders assemble for a briefing, while everyone else gathers their equipment.

The most important piece of equipment—and the primary weapon for HRT operators—is the HK MP5 submachine gun with a collapsible stock. Developed in the 1960s by a team of German engineers, the MP5 has become an "industry standard," used by more than 40 nations and numerous military, law enforcement, and security organizations. The MP5 has been specially modified for HRT purposes with laser-aiming devices, tactical front-facing lights, and pistol grips on the forward part of the gun.

The men may also carry Remington M870 12-gauge shotguns. These pump-action weapons have barrels in several lengths, pistol grips, and feature rails for mounting accessories such as lights and *foregrips*. In one variation, the M870p "Masterkey" system, a cut-down version of the M870 is mounted beneath the barrel of a conventional M4 or M16 assault rifle. That system provides deadly force for the operator in CQC and helps retain the MP5's value as an automatic weapon. In another variation, the weapon is loaded with special breaching rounds to blow

SWAT team members use headsets for communication and ballistic shields for added cover.

Hallways can be dangerous because of the limited maneuverability they allow. Operators often blow holes in walls so that they can move from room to room in greater safety.

away door hinges and locks.

HRT's secondary armament for many years was the Springfield Armory's M1911A1 .45 caliber pistol, based on a design dating back to 1911 but still noted for its reliability. It has begun to be phased out by Glock 22 and Glock 23 *polymer* pistols.

The men wear flame-retardant suits and gloves, heavy boots, and thick plastic kneepads. Everyone has a Kevlar helmet and goggles strong enough to withstand blast pressures and to protect the eyes from flying debris. They wear bulletproof vests that have external webbing for carrying pouches filled with extra ammunition, and any other gear depends on the profile of the mission at hand. There's also room on the vests for medical packs and—setting HRT apart from the long-ago demonstration by Delta Force—handcuffs.

Radios are an essential element of HRT gear so that the team members can stay in touch with each other during the chaos of an assault. If the situation they are responding to may involve weapons of mass destruction (WMD), they have gas masks equipped with valves to enable them to drink liquids and enhanced voice box amplifiers to maintain communication.

Since many operations involve smashing down doors, the team is equipped with battering rams and collapsible sledgehammers. Another key piece of assault gear is the Halligan bar. Named for the New York City firefighter who invented it in the late 1940s, the device is commonly described as a "crowbar on steroids." Varying in length from 18 inches to more than 4 feet (46–122 cm), the bar is forked at one end, with a heavy blade and a tapered point at the other.

Once their gear is ready, the men attend a meeting that outlines the objectives and rules of the upcoming mission. When that's over, everyone helps load gear such as tents, food, electric generators, lanterns, and an array of other equipment onto trucks. They then head to Andrews Air Force Base to board an

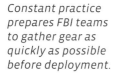

Constant practice prepares FBI teams to gather gear as quickly as possible before deployment.

awaiting transport aircraft—usually a C-130 Hercules or C-141 Starlifter.

By the time the operators arrive, larger vehicles have already been loaded into the aircraft. Because of their long practice and experience in fast deployments, the team is almost always "wheels up" within four hours of receiving The Call. As Christopher Whitcomb, who made many such flights, notes, "The four-engine jet aircraft sagged under the weight of HRT and its support staff, their gear, a four-wheel-drive van containing a remote control robot, the Chevy Suburban ambulance, a four-wheel-drive box truck, and the MD-530 helicopter."

Once aloft, the men settle in for what is often several hours of discomfort. Most operators have to wear earplugs to combat the roar of the engines. They sit rigidly on narrow canvas benches bolted to each side of the aircraft, their knees jammed against some large piece of equipment. Without windows, it's hard to gauge progress. On top of everything else, it's not uncommon for air traffic controllers to route HRT flights into areas of turbulence so that commercial flights can take advantage of the smoothest air.

Since many HRT flights take place at night, operators are likely to be sleep-deprived when they arrive on-scene. However, their training kicks in and overrides any sense of fatigue. The airplane has barely stopped moving when the team unloads it, climbs into transport vehicles, and speeds to the incident site.

While most of its operations take place inside the U.S., HRT sometimes ventures overseas. The team provided security for then FBI director Louis Freeh during a visit to Israel in 1995. Another group helped apprehend Mohamed Rashed Daoud Al-Owhali, who was wanted in connection with terrorist bombings in Kenya and Tanzania in 1998 that killed 324 and

From combat missions to special ops, the C-130 Hercules is known for its versatility.

Osama bin Laden helped finance the 1998 bombing of the U.S. embassy in Nairobi, Kenya.

wounded thousands more. Still others traveled to war-torn Kosovo in 1999 to provide security for FBI agents looking for evidence of war crimes committed during the conflict that had begun the previous year and was recently concluded. In 2011, HRT operators played key roles after the hijacking of the American yacht *S/V Quest* by Somali pirates. While the four hostages were killed before they could be rescued, the operators took the lead in compiling evidence to use in court against the pirates.

With the widespread publicity the unit has received, it isn't surprising that HRT appears often in popular media. One of the more notable mentions came in best-selling thriller author David Baldacci's 2001 novel *Last Man Standing*, in which an HRT unit is ambushed. A character named Web London is the only survivor, and he must overcome the suspicions of fellow agents who believe he froze up at the critical moment. Baldacci wanted to give as accurate a picture of HRT as possible. "I visited the HRT's headquarters, toured the facilities, spent time with HRT operators, asked a zillion questions, read everything I could find on them," Baldacci said in an interview for Readersread.com. "I really wanted to get into their heads and hearts to bring it all to life on the pages. I think I succeeded.... I learned to ride a horse and fired machine guns, among other activities, while researching *Last Man Standing*." Reviewers and readers agreed. *Publishers Weekly* called it "Baldacci's most accomplished thriller," and the novel made it to the *New York Times* list of best-selling books.

HRT sometimes appears in the novels of best-selling author Tom Clancy. Clancy's books are noted for their extreme realism, and he sought the same effect in video games based on the exploits of HRT. Clancy helped Red Storm Entertainment develop the Rainbow Six series of tactical shooter games in the 1990s. The games feature operators who rescue hostages and take out terrorists. Clancy originally modeled the operators after HRT but changed the game's characters to an international team to broaden its appeal worldwide. In 2003, GameCube released the video-game version of Clancy's 1991 novel *The Sum of All Fears*. In it, players command HRT units with a variety of armaments in 11 different scenarios, all with the goal of preventing the release of a dangerous weapon on American soil. "For more than 15 years, Tom Clancy has presented the gritty, realistic counterpoint to most action games' abstract ideal of combat," gaming writer Joe Keiser summarized in 2012. "You could bleed out from a single bullet wound. Reflexes would rarely play a role in victory. Instead, success would come from careful operations, selection of *ordnance*, and the Planning Stage, a pre-battle strategizing session that let you lay out the positions and pathing of your computer-controlled operatives."

State law enforcement agencies often cooperate and train with FBI SWAT teams.

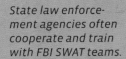

FORCE FACTS Units often leave Quantico and travel to other parts of the country to train in environments such as mountains, deserts, and large seaports that can't be duplicated at the Academy.

HRT AND SWAT IN ACTION

WHILE SPEAKING SPECIFICALLY ABOUT NEGOTIATORS SUCH as himself, longtime FBI agent Gary Noesner undoubtedly expressed the feelings of HRT members as well when he said, "I've gone into every situation wanting to see the person do what I think is in their best interest, which is put their weapon down ... and surrender peacefully." Despite this goal and HRT's overall success rate, two of the unit's highest-profile operations ended badly when their targets refused to "surrender peacefully." The negative outcome provoked severe criticism, which led to changes being made in the structuring of HRT's overall command and in some of the unit's operational procedures.

The first incident began in August 1992 when federal marshals tried to serve an arrest warrant on Idaho survivalist and former Army Special Forces operator Randy Weaver at his cabin deep in a forested area known as Ruby Ridge. Weaver had been charged with federal weapons violations. Deeply mistrustful of the government, Weaver didn't appear in court to answer the charges. The U.S. Marshals Service declared him a dangerous fugitive as a result. Before trying to arrest Weaver, the marshals put the cabin under surveillance. An accidental confrontation led to the shooting deaths of Weaver's 14-year-old son Samuel and a marshal. The marshals then asked HRT for help.

Under standard FBI *Rules of Engagement* (ROE), agents

After the Ruby Ridge standoff, federal agents gathered evidence from the Weaver cabin.

FORCE FACTS In the past 20 years, women have become increasingly a part of SWAT teams, a reflection of the FBI's growing emphasis on recruiting women to serve as agents.

cannot use deadly force against anyone, unless they are acting in self-defense or if they believe that the life of another person is in imminent danger. In addition, they are required to issue verbal warnings before using deadly force.

Based on the confrontation that had killed Samuel Weaver and the marshal, as well as reports that the Weavers had fired on a helicopter carrying TV journalist Geraldo Rivera, the ROE at Ruby Ridge were different. Agents were authorized to open fire if they saw an adult carrying a weapon, as long as no children were at risk. They were not obligated to issue a verbal warning before firing. Acting under that modified set of ROE, an HRT sniper shot Weaver in the back as he, his daughter, and a friend—who were all carrying rifles—crossed the yard to a shed where Samuel's body was lying. As the three people fled back to the house, the sniper fired another round. It wounded the friend and killed Weaver's wife Vicki, who was holding her 10-month-old daughter and standing behind the front door—where she was invisible to the sniper. The bloody incident aroused public outcry. While Weaver was charged with multiple crimes, his only conviction was for his failure to appear in court. A senate committee eventually decided that the shooting of Vicki Weaver was unjustified. The sniper was *indicted* for manslaughter several years later, but the charges were eventually dropped.

Rudy Ridge was still fresh in the national consciousness when HRT became involved in another controversial operation the following February in Waco, Texas. Agents of the Bureau of Alcohol, Tobacco, Firearms and Explosives (ATF) tried to use a search warrant to access the grounds of a compound belonging to a small religious group called the Branch Davidians in February 1993. The agency believed that the group had been purchasing and stockpiling illegal weapons and ammunition. There were also reports of drug manufacturing and child abuse.

Like Randy Weaver, Branch Davidian leader David Koresh

HRT agents are trained to aim precisely and hold their fire until commanded.

was geared up for a fight. A TV reporter inadvertently tipped off Koresh that ATF was coming. In the 45-minute firefight that ensued, 4 ATF agents were killed, while the others were forced to retreat. Six Branch Davidians also died, and dozens on both sides were wounded.

Once again, HRT was summoned. A series of fruitless negotiations began, with each side accusing the other of acting in bad faith. At the same time, HRT employed psychological devices designed to deprive the Branch Davidians of sleep and make them more willing to surrender. These tactics included having low-flying helicopters hover over the compound, shining bright searchlights through the windows, and playing loud rock-and-roll music continuously. Nothing worked, though, and the siege dragged on for nearly two months. Finally, the team launched an assault. While it's still not clear who was responsible, a fire that engulfed the compound broke out and led to the deaths of 76 Branch Davidians. The case remains controversial today.

While most high-profile cases feature HRT, sometimes FBI SWAT teams "take point" instead. One notable example of this occurred on August 3, 2011, in Mosman, Australia, a wealthy suburb of Sydney. Eighteen-year-old Madeleine Pulver was alone in her home. Suddenly, a masked man later identified as Paul Peters broke in and threatened her with a baseball bat. Then he chained a black box around Madeleine's neck and left a ransom note that included an e-mail address by which he could be reached. Part of the note read, "Plastic explosives are located inside the small black combination case delivered to you." The note added that the case was booby-trapped and would explode if anyone tried to remove it.

When the man scuttled away, Madeleine called her father for help. He called the police,

In 2000, an official report cleared FBI agents of responsibility in the Waco fire of 1993.

who responded with a bomb squad. Madeleine endured nine frightening hours before the squad determined that the bomb didn't contain explosives. What was quickly dubbed the "Collar Bomb Case" attracted worldwide attention.

Starting with the e-mail address Peters had provided, authorities tracked him to a house near Louisville, Kentucky. An FBI SWAT team was dispatched to the address. According to one of Peters's neighbors in what was normally a very quiet neighborhood, the team "came in heavy and hard.... We had guys with machine guns in our back yard," the neighbor said.

The men's training paid off, as their overwhelming force took Peters completely by surprise and captured him without firing any shots. He was *extradited* to Australia and sentenced to 13 and a half years in prison.

Often, SWAT and HRT work together. In early 1988, a man named Charlie Leaf tracked his ex-girlfriend Cheryl Hart and their four-year-old son to her parents' house in Connecticut. They had moved there to escape Leaf's constant abuse. Though he nearly killed Hart and the boy on the spot, she talked him

In the event of a crisis, a local field office SWAT team will act as a first responder.

into driving away with them.

Hart's parents alerted the FBI. Within hours, the Richmond, Virginia, field office SWAT team had tracked Leaf and his captives to a small farmhouse near Sperryville. When the team entered the house that night, Leaf threatened to kill Hart and their son. The agents backed away, and negotiations began. According to FBI agent Kevin August, Leaf's demands included safe passage to "somewhere south where there were mountains" in the FBI helicopter that had landed nearby.

After hours of negotiation, the FBI came to the conclusion that no matter what they did, Leaf intended to kill both his hostages. They decided to take him out, and HRT sniper teams were deployed near the house. The FBI allowed Leaf to see them loading the helicopter with the supplies he had demanded. He emerged from the house using Hart as a human shield, holding a knife to her throat and a gun to her head. He had tied the terrified boy to his shoulders. Leaf's head was too close to Hart's for the snipers to risk a shot. The helicopter lifted off as Leaf approached, stirring up dust and leaves to distract him. At the same time, HRT agents set off stun grenades. Leaf dropped to his knees and whispered, "Goodbye, Kitten," fully intending to kill Hart. But his change in position allowed a sniper to gain a clear shot in the split second before Leaf could pull the trigger. The crisis over, both hostages left the scene unharmed.

It was yet another example of how HRT lives up to its motto and validation of the group's key role in the American system of criminal justice—a role that former member Jaime Atherton notes was by no means a slam dunk in its early days. "You've got to remember that in 1983 when it started, there were a lot of people who said, 'As soon as the Olympics are over, you guys are going to be reassigned,'" Atherton reported.

Obviously the "guys" were not reassigned. And today, there are countless people who are glad they were not. HRT continues to prove its worth in high-risk situations, and it is poised to continue its mission in the years to come.

The FBI, headquartered in Washington, D.C., employs more than 35,000 worldwide.

★ ★ ★

FORCE FACTS Former Navy SEAL and Medal of Honor winner Thomas Norris lost an eye in the Vietnam War and became the only HRT member to operate with just one eye.

When not in the field, HRT and SWAT teams keep up a rigorous practice regimen.

100 CRTG
LINK
BLANK

FORCE FACTS HRT operators commonly fire a thousand rounds of ammunition or even more every week so they can keep their shooting skills at the highest possible level.

GLOSSARY

U.S. SPECIAL FORCES

breaching – breaking through a barrier

cache – a concealed storage location

casualty – a person injured or killed in an accident or a battle

cyanide – a toxic salt used as a poison

deploying – moving personnel into position for military action

extradited – took a suspect from one state or country to another to stand trial

fast-roping – sliding down a thick rope suspended from a helicopter as rapidly as possible

foregrips – handles of a weapon mounted under the front part of the barrel

indicted – charged with a crime

magazines – containers in guns that hold bullets and allow them to be fed into the firing chamber

Nomex – a lightweight, flame-resistant artificial fiber used in protective clothing for firefighters and other workers in hazardous situations

ordnance – military or law enforcement weapons, ammunition, and related equipment

polymer – a form of plastic noted for its exceptional strength

rappelling – descending a vertical surface using a rope coiled around the body and attached at a higher point

reconnaissance – a search to gain information, usually conducted in secret

Rules of Engagement – rules under which government forces can operate in conflict situations; these rules include but are not limited to the application of lethal force

tango – a code word representing the letter *T*, sometimes used as a name for "terrorist"

white supremacists – people who believe that white-skinned people are superior to people of other racial backgrounds

FORCE FACTS In the winter of 1996, HRT went directly from one operation in Puerto Rico to another in Michigan, undergoing a 125-degree temperature swing in less than 12 hours.

SELECTED BIBLIOGRAPHY

Ackerman, Thomas H. *FBI Careers: The Ultimate Guide to Landing a Job as One of America's Finest*. Indianapolis: JIST Works, 2010.

Coulson, Danny, and Elaine Shannon. *No Heroes: Inside the FBI's Secret Counter-Terror Force*. New York: Pocket Books, 1999.

Kessler, Ronald. *Bureau: The Secret History of the FBI*. New York: St. Martin's Press, 2002.

Noesner, Gary. *Stalling for Time: My Life as an FBI Hostage Negotiator*. New York: Random House, 2010.

Pushies, Fred. *U.S. Counter-Terrorist Forces*. St. Paul, Minn.: MBI Publishing, 2002.

Theoharis, Athan G., ed. *The FBI: A Comprehensive Reference Guide*. New York: The Oryx Press, 2000.

Van Sandt, Clint, with Daniel Paisner. *Facing Down Evil: Life on the Edge as an FBI Hostage Negotiator*. New York: G. P. Putnam's Sons, 2006.

Whitcomb, Christopher. *Cold Zero: Inside the FBI Hostage Rescue Team*. New York: Warner Books, 2001.

WEBSITES

The Hostage Rescue Team
http://www.fbi.gov/news/stories/2013/february/the-hostage-rescue-team-30-years-of-service

An ongoing series beginning on the 30th anniversary of HRT covers its history, training, notable missions, and more.

"Stalling for Time" with an FBI Hostage Negotiator
http://www.npr.org/templates/story/story.php?storyId=130103016

A National Public Radio story about the Leaf hostage situation, including the link to the original radio broadcast.

READ MORE

Brush, Jim. *Special Forces*. Mankato, Minn.: Sea-to-Sea, 2012.

Cooper, Jason. *U.S. Special Operations*. Vero Beach, Fla.: Rourke, 2004.

Note: Every effort has been made to ensure that the websites listed above have educational value and that they contain no inappropriate material. However, because of the nature of the Internet, it is impossible to guarantee that these sites will remain active indefinitely or that their contents will not be altered.

INDEX

U.S. SPECIAL FORCES